Let the Dance Begin

Praise for *Let the Dance Begin*

"This is amazing! I have known Peter Jain since his childhood. He was an "A+" Music Theory student of mine at Humboldt State University. It is a real pleasure to recommend his excellent literary skill as well as these beautiful photographs of Humboldt."

— CHARLES L. MOON, Humboldt State University Professor Emeritus of Music Theory, Photographer, & Gemstone Faceter

"Peter Jain's tale of Terpsichore is told with delicate elegance, finding color and creative movement in the commonplace as thought and image meld into a memorable reflection on motion."

—KEVIN HOOVER, Journalist, Artist, Musician, & Hiker

"These words and images capture the extraordinary healing power of Northern Humboldt's natural beauty. Thank you, Peter Jain, for sharing this very touching, personal journey!"

— JANDY BERGMANN, MFA, GCFP, Humboldt State University Lecturer of Theater, Film, & Dance

"Ah! Wonderful! A heart full, artful, weaving of images and words that will challenge and awaken you, inspire and invite you…to remember…to embrace…the beauty and the love dancing all around us in Nature and in each and everyone. Yea! Love. Thank you. I am so grateful." — LAMA THUBTEN GONPO TSERING

Let the Dance Begin

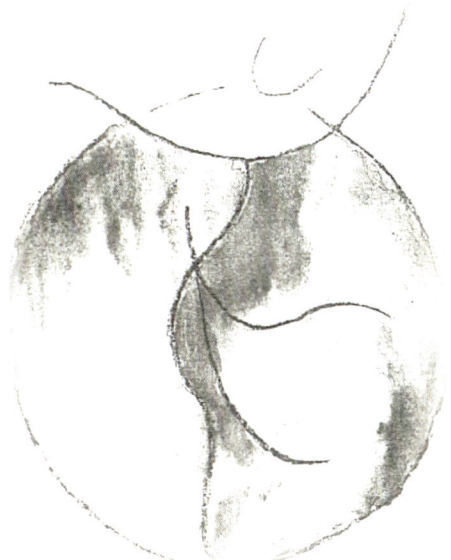

GREETINGS FROM HUMBOLDT

Peter K. Jain

Wild Earth Press

Let the Dance Begin

Text Copyright © 2014 by Peter Jain

Photographs copyright © 2014 in the names of the individual photographers as noted specifically on pages 78-81, which constitute an extension of this page.

All rights reserved.

No part of this publication may be reproduced, stored in or introduced into a retrieval system, or transmitted, in any form, or by any means, electronic, mechanical, photocopying, recording, or otherwise, without the prior written permission of the copyright owner. To request permission, please contact: wildearthpress@gmail.com.

Published by WILD EARTH PRESS
P.O. Box 15
Arcata, CA 95518
www.wildearthpress.com

Cover Design
by CM Phillips & Kerima Furniss
Cover Photo by Peter K Jain
Author Photo by CM Phillips
Interior Design and Editing by CM Phillips
Set in Palatino & Sylfaen Type

Publisher's Cataloging-in-Publication data
Jain, Peter K.
Let the dance begin : greetings from Humboldt / Peter K. Jain. —1st ed.
p.   cm.

ISBN 978-0-9894550-3-9 (hardcover.)
ISBN 978-0-9894550-2-2 (pbk.)
1. Humboldt County (Calif.) —Pictorial works. 2. Poetry — Humboldt County (Calif.). 3. Nature, healing power of — Poetry. I. Title.
PS3519.A457 L4 2014
979.412—dc22
2014935219

Printed in England.
Proudly printed on FSC certified, 100% recycled paper using soy/vegetable-based inks.

DEDICATION

This book is dedicated to both of my children: my daughter, Elyse Louisa Pickart-Jain, during whose first months of life this text was written and completed on July 17, 2001, and to her brother, David Wilder Pickart-Jain, whose sudden death on March 10, 2013 brought the impulse to carry this work to print.

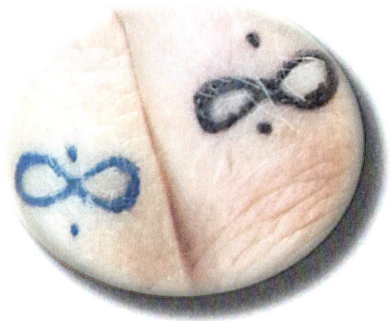

"It is music and dancing that make me at peace with the world."
— NELSON MANDELA

ACKNOWLEDGMENTS

I would like to thank Michael and Kerima Furniss of Wild Earth Press for their kind and generous assistance on this project, and I would also like to express my deep gratitude to CM Phillips; without her graphic design, photography and editorial skills, as well as her support, advice, and encouragment, this book never would have made it to print.

Let the Dance Begin

GREETINGS FROM HUMBOLDT

"Dance is the hidden language of the soul."
— *MARTHA GRAHAM*

INTRODUCTION

Imagine a world without beauty...

No, it's just too harsh to do!

The task at hand is to write an introduction, to say why this was written, this volume of words called *Let the Dance Begin*. The answer has something to do with beauty. Sometimes we are drawn to things we don't know why, and beauty can have something to do with it. The spring of 2001 was a kind of dance with beauty. In April of that year my daughter, Elyse, was born, and things seemed especially beautiful. I was taking a dance class where we were urged to write in a weekly journal. The weeks of dancing with writing (especially after middle-of-the-night bottle feedings) brought forth a series of images and impressions from growing up here on the north coast of California, our beautiful region. *Let the Dance Begin* was written at that time. But why bring it to print now, with greetings from Humboldt?

If a visitor were to ask, "What is life like here?" well, this writing is a small description, a little world in minature. To me the people of our area are a reflection of its natural beauty. All of us are earth lovers, nature enthusiasts, seekers and creators to some degree. There is something primal and healing in artistic creation, in setting aside day-to-day cares and losing oneself in the pursuit of beauty. Everybody is an artist, at least an amateur one. Some people here even make their living by art. Either way, working with beauty has its own rewards. It is a natural and harmless pastime, seeking contact with beauty. People all over do it in a million different ways. And people have for centuries. In the end I have to agree with examples of humanity such as Henry David Thoreau and John Muir for saying such things as, "Everybody needs beauty as well as bread" (Muir).

Humor me please as I write that for better or worse, I am a product of our area, this region populated by beauty seekers. It was Muir who also said, "An early morning walk is a blessing for the whole day."

Our natural area here is rich with walkers and runners and hikers and bikers, birders and surfers and swimmers of rivers, dippers in creeks and deep sea divers, not to mention rock climbers and hang gliders; kayakers, canoeists, wind surfers and sailors, all enjoying their dance with nature. We have poets and puppeteers and performers for pleasure, musicians and minstrels and jewelers of leisure; our samba and other bands are a local treasure, using love as the grease to increase peace beyond measure. We have rock hounds and masons and sculptors galore, and people who stack stones down by the shore, dancers at the beach around blazing bonfires, and climbers of trees who go even higher, pickers of mushrooms, of herbs and of berries, diggers of clams and milkers of dairies, gardeners and farmers of food **AND** of beauty, doing their work and enjoying their duty, cooks and bakers and brewers of brew, knitters and weavers of old with the new, composers, builders, collageurs, and shapers, wood workers and those who make art folding papers. We have chainsaw artists and creators of kinetic contraptions, living their purpose through artistic abstractions, and if that's not enough, we have body healers; masseuses; glass, tile, paint and clay throwers; jokers and jugglers and bubble gum blowers.

Forgive me, sometimes I get carried away by a moment of enthusiasm.

Thinking back now, the year 2001 began as an optimistic time. The 20th century of so many wars was behind us. The possibilities of human realization seemed closer, and a new era was at hand. Then came the terrorist attacks of September 11th; things changed; we did the best we could. These pages of writing about dance were set aside. Looking at them thirteen years later, they still seem true enough; though, I wouldn't write them now.

Sometimes we are drawn to things we don't know why. Last year (2013) my son, David, was struck dead by a car while walking across a street in Eureka. Peace and blessings be with him as I honor his dear life and those who were fortunate enough to have known him. Out of my grief and upheaval came a greater appreciation for beauty all around. A first-time interest arose in me to use a camera while seeking healing outdoors. The photos I took brought back the images of dance and nature from thirteen years ago. With the addition of photographs taken by my partner in love, Cyndy Phillips, and one salmon photo by Thomas Dunklin, we have this hopeful volume created around the birth of my daughter, Elyse, and the death of my son, David.

Let the Dance Begin, GREETINGS FROM HUMBOLDT.

It is my hope that this work will be of benefit to people. After all, isn't that something of our purpose in life? The proceeds from the first year of sales will go towards bringing a Tibetan Buddhist teacher, Geshe Lobsang Tenkyong, to Humboldt County. Geshe escaped from Tibet as a child and has studied and taught under the direction of the Dalai Lama in India, Nepal, and Italy. It seems to me that people all around the globe are crying out, working and praying to help make the world a healthier and more peaceful place. *Let the Dance Begin,* GREETINGS FROM HUMBOLDT is my effort.

Thank you, you have done so much for me.

Peter K. Jain (March 22, 2014)

"With our thoughts, we create our world."
—HIS HOLINESS THE 14TH DALAI LAMA, Opening Prayer to the U.S. Senate, March 6, 2014

"On with the dance! Let joy be unrestrained."
— *LORD BYRON*

Let the Dance Begin

"Be embraced, millions!
 This kiss to the entire wold!"
— FRIEDRICH SCHILLER, "Ode to Joy"

Let the dance begin,
Let the dance of freedom begin.
Friends, Dancers,
Let the life-dance of freedom begin!

Ah ha, let's see that it's here already,
Waiting, nearly hidden and obscured
By machinery of our own making.

Let us observe the ceaseless dance,
Sometimes fitful, even stilted and awkward,
Yet still a natural way,
The spirit dance, the earth dance,
An ongoing affair of movement and mystery.

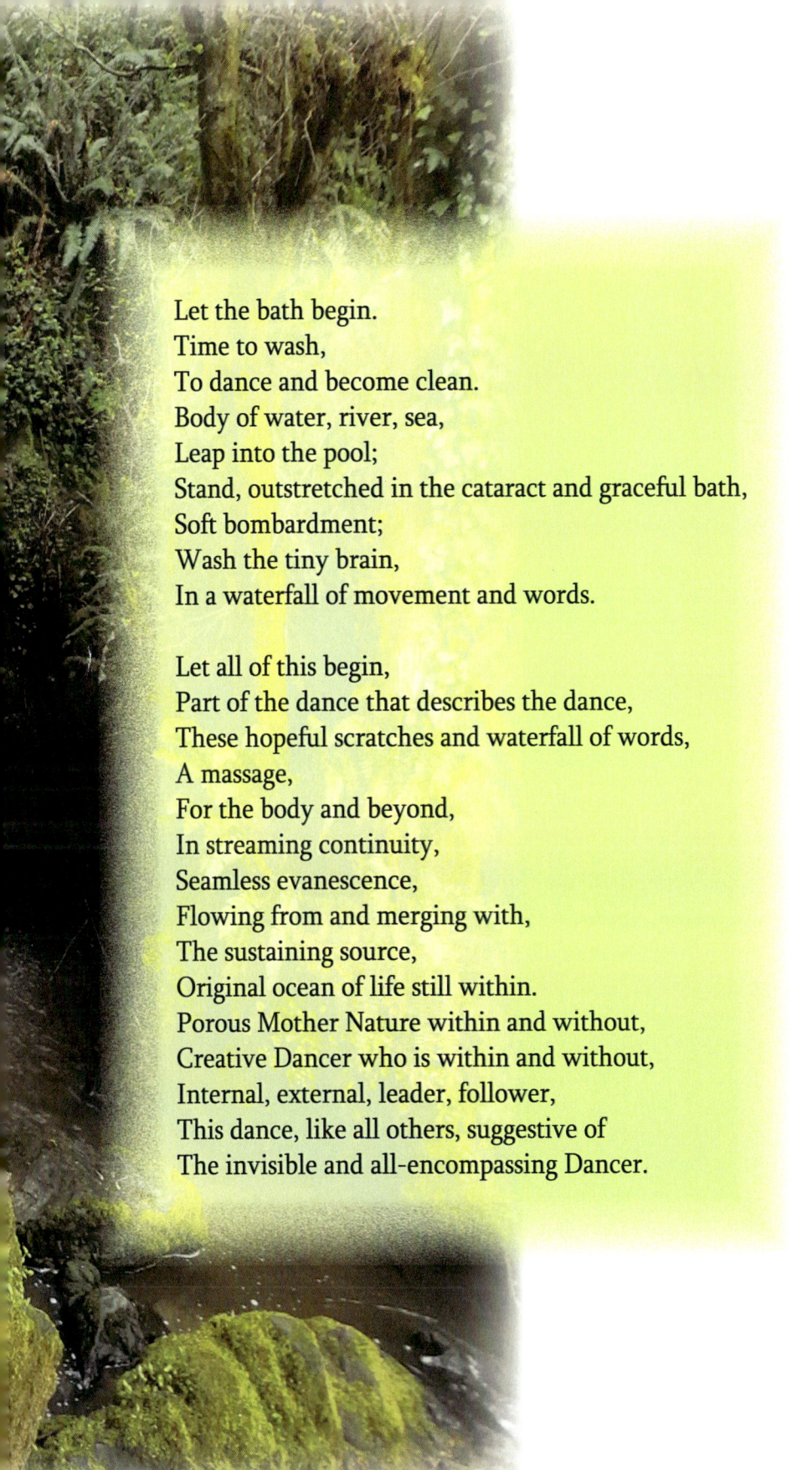

Let the bath begin.
Time to wash,
To dance and become clean.
Body of water, river, sea,
Leap into the pool;
Stand, outstretched in the cataract and graceful bath,
Soft bombardment;
Wash the tiny brain,
In a waterfall of movement and words.

Let all of this begin,
Part of the dance that describes the dance,
These hopeful scratches and waterfall of words,
A massage,
For the body and beyond,
In streaming continuity,
Seamless evanescence,
Flowing from and merging with,
The sustaining source,
Original ocean of life still within.
Porous Mother Nature within and without,
Creative Dancer who is within and without,
Internal, external, leader, follower,
This dance, like all others, suggestive of
The invisible and all-encompassing Dancer.

I am you and you are me,
Watching faithfully.
Mirror of water, river, sea.
I am you and you are me,
Watching faithfully,
From within and close by,
Cleansed,
With first-time freshness,
And loveliness,
Observing our reflected echo,
Our perennial beauty.

On this morn,
A new dance form is born.
Neither you before
Nor I before,
Washing, we enter the dance
That never was before,
The ongoing dance that leaves us clean.

Let the unstoppable force of life
Begin breathing and pulsing,
Swinging,
Tickling and chuckling,
Twitching and tadpole wriggling,
In its purpose and play.

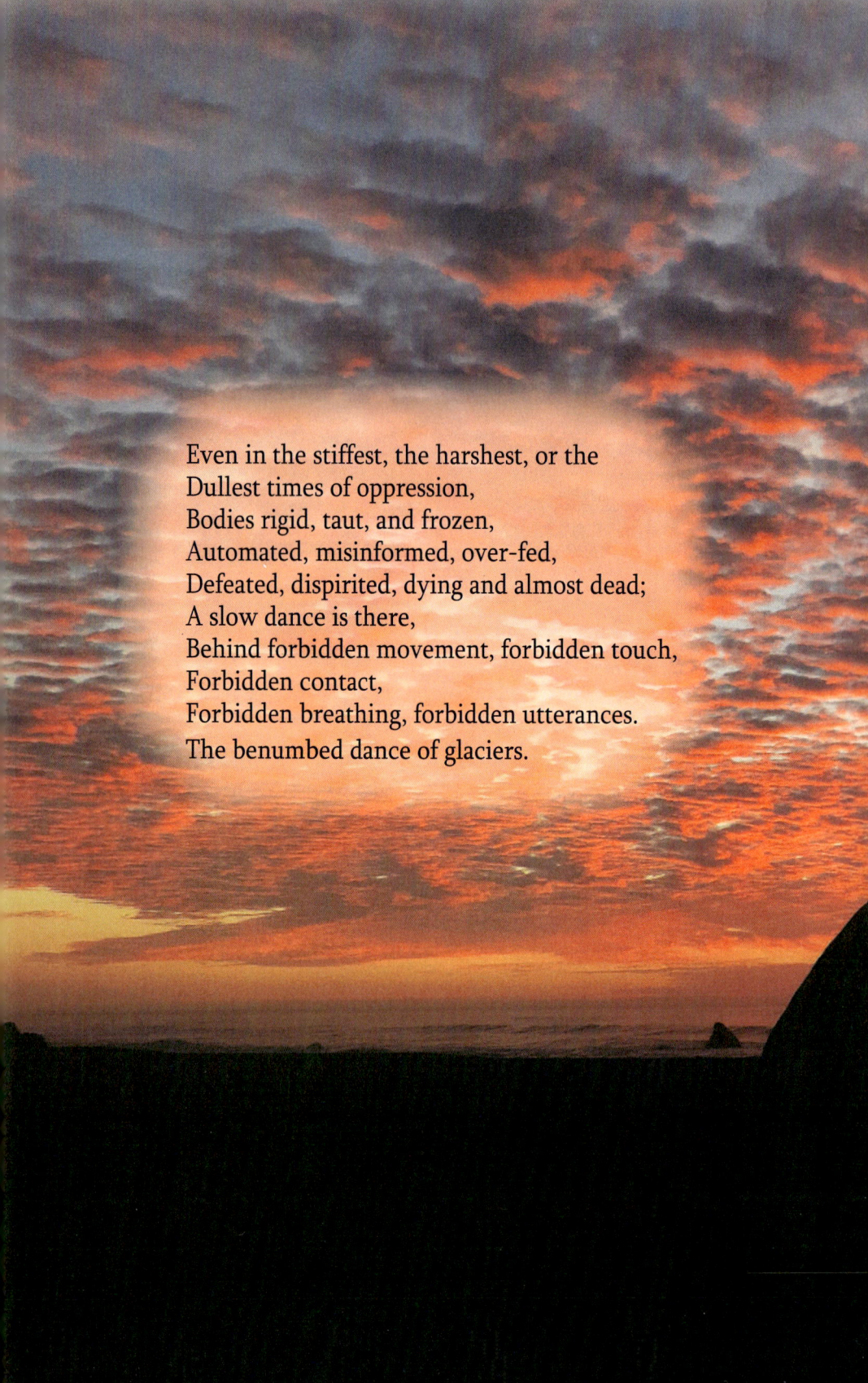

Even in the stiffest, the harshest, or the
Dullest times of oppression,
Bodies rigid, taut, and frozen,
Automated, misinformed, over-fed,
Defeated, dispirited, dying and almost dead;
A slow dance is there,
Behind forbidden movement, forbidden touch,
Forbidden contact,
Forbidden breathing, forbidden utterances.
The benumbed dance of glaciers.

Were you mistreated?
Punished, beaten, humiliated, captured,
Stepped on,
Forced to submit?
Lied to, disappointed, dispossessed?
Neglected, deprived?
Slighted, belittled, insulted, made fun of?
Made to keep still to the point of disappearing
(Is that what we were made for?)
Tyrannized, colonized, relocated,
Violated, slaughtered, annihilated, exterminated?
Compelled, conscripted,
Put to work, reduced to slavery?
Did this happen to us?
Did we do it to others?

It's not a surprise that we are a little tense,
That we are a little stiff and wooden in our
body-dance.
Frightening and hungry ghosts are with us,
Disposing us towards being our own oppressors
And unknowingly enslaving us, our brute
selves,
To the false authority
Of the restless and fearful mind in frozen body.
Our task, to grope our way,
Through this vapor.
To fall and swim and crawl,
Our true way,
Through darkness.
To rise and frolic freely,

Unstoppably, among the veils of ignorance.

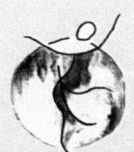

Freedom.

A piece of paper declares our independence,
Our equality, our autonomy, liberty, life, and happiness.
The document,
A written expression of
Inborn freedom stating its claim,
Freedom that requires more than someone else's guarantee,
That requires each individual to win it, to earn it,
To struggle for it, to dance for it!
No one else can do it for us.
No one else will do it for us.

Confront your freedom.
Surrender yourself to it.

There is no authority greater than you,
Though we are nothing without our teachers,
Those who have generously served us by leading us.

Everything according to its nature to be of service,
Enriching and uplifting the lives of others.
We, all of us, are teachers;
There is no choice in this.
It is a fact of existence.

Young one, free spirit,
Never give away your allegiance,
Your allegiance to conscience.
Call it freedom, or obedience — it is the same.
Inner voice,
The way,
Live by supple conscience.
And be sustained.

But remain watchful,
In your lively prance,
For there are those who wait
To bring you down.
Growl them away in your darkest dance.
With claws and knife-like teeth,
Send them packing!

Even while sleeping
One must not forsake one's allegiance,
The loyalty to what one knows is true and must be.

The slumbering sleepwalker
Dream-dancers in darkness,
Life-force unblinking, untiring, unabated,
Ever seeking true health and wholeness.

Behold the netherworld:
Dead piles of skeletons, and
skulls, and souls,
A cave dance,
Of terrifying specters and phantasms,
Vying and trying to get a hold!
Vice-like grip of unspeakable horror,
Of inescapable terror,
Slashing,
Brutal, violent, and vicious,
Authoritarian,
And fearful,
Lashing and gnashing,
Knives and broken pieces of glass,
Another human sacrifice.
Let me go!

But there is no escape,
Only temporary induced plague relief
By running from the nightmare.

Me, the roused sleeper,
Drone, not yet ready to dance with death,
Only dimly aware of the dark underworld
Dance drama of demons, each night in dreams.

By day patiently continuing to sleepmarch
through the years.

Are you constrained in your dance?
As I am?
A little nervous?
Critical, self-conscious, mistrustful,
Self-persecuting, self-condemning?
How could one condemn oneself?
And yet it happens all the time.
Condemned to death.

Fear of strangers?
Are we concealing ourselves in cautionary fear?

Come out in the truth and dance.
Let us wake up together and dance in daylight,
For soon the dancer will die.
There is no security in the sidelines.
Grieve away the unlived life, of death before its time.
Get on with it, take courage, take flight.

How is trust created, how is it broken?
Is it possible, despite harm, to bear no malice?
How is trust renewed?
To dance again.

Have we been able to rely on the world thus far?
Bear witness to the truth,
The selfless and bountiful munificence of the
sun and the earth,
Patiently bestowing faithful and undying
blessings,
The seasons, the rhythms, the swinging ebbs
and tides.

The small and deluded have tried to grasp the earth.
Do you reject this sentence?
I, myself, have attempted to subjugate and own the earth,
And will do so again...
Partially realizing my quest,
I have unknowingly defeated and subjugated myself
In ever-widening circles of protection,
A grasping disembodied mind reigning supreme over flawed surroundings,
Broken off, alienated, stranger to myself,
Out of sorts, mistrustful, fearful, deadened, and unloving,
Vaguely uneasy and incomplete,
Barren in the fruitless search,
And the insistence in finding what it is I want,
Somewhere out there where I expect it to be.

Now I will speak to you.
Please take it in the way that it is intended.
Time has come to choose your body,
Your authentic and complete blood-and-guts self.
Muscles and bone,
Face and skin,
Integrated with all aspects of being,
The intrinsic value of one's necessary body,
One's necessary nature, and one's necessary planetary species.

We must die
To the notion that the world is separate from ourselves.
Unbroken whole,
Self-mirroring,
Unity of life.

This is our new millennium lesson and task,
To learn the truth of the body,
The truth of nature,
And the truth of spirit,
Work long neglected and long feared,
Late begun and never concluded,
Sides of the same thing,
Facets of the same diamond life-jewel,
Millennium exploration,
Our creative, meaningful work.

Is it possible to recognize the richness of our
reflected inner and outer life?
To value our wealthy and generous planet,
To value our equally abundant interior world,
As co-participants in the earth-dance?
Beautiful and varied landscape,
Matching our
Beautiful and varied inscape.

Begin,
And behold,
The wild earth-dance:
Of vibrating mounds of red ants,
Over writhing earthworms in the fertile,
turning soil.
Or behold the swing dance of one, solitary,
upright, quivering blade of fescue.
Or the united swaying of endless prairie grasses,
forerunners of the coming thunderstorm.

Or of bison hunkered against the bitterest of
snow flurries.
Of wild mustangs, or hoary mountain goats,
Head-butting their way through life.

Or of leaping salmon desirous of completing
their cycle, their ritual, their fulfillment,
Weaving, threading, nuzzling ahead,
Obdurate in their final intention,
Through currents of swiftly streaming rivers of
clear water,
Surrounded by undeniable, yet benign,
resistance
That is as invisible to them
As is the presence of a fresh breeze drifting
through the trees.

Behold the flocks of shorebirds flying like
wind waves in effortless synchronization.
Or migratory songbirds skipping and skittering
their continental rounds.
With graceful geese above
Following their similar returns and rounds.
And the spiraling, soaring condor,
Spinning and threading his rhythms and rounds.

Romping bear cubs, frisking coyote pups,
hopping kangaroo mice.
Or a company of bobbing and nodding penguins
on the ice floe.
Or paddling sea turtles, pulsating jelly fish, and
Enormous whales plunging to unfathomable
depths.

Or huge herds of caribou, buffalo, or elk,
Sweeping to the left and right of land masses.
Land masses themselves drifting through the oceans
And dancing unrestrained to their own inner rhythm.
The surface of the sea doing its own unquenchable dance,
Waves releasing on the shore,
The unceasing nudging and shuffling of surf pebbles.

An entire ocean made to polish a single exquisite beach agate.

These revelries, and other unnumbered dances
of peace,
Are in and around all of us:
Rivers of red salt-watered, heart-driven
blood corpuscles
Swimming and lilting through our veins
and organs
And schools of teeming tropical coral fishes,
Glide-dancing a stately and tranquil,
Chaconne of the undersea world.
While on the mountaintop,
Resting pure and motionless,
Is the magnificent montane still life dance,
Resplendent with lichens whose colors span
an inconceivable palette,
Stationary sculpted dwarf trees, and the tiniest,
most delightful alpine flowers,
Pristinely arranged by an unseen hand.
And in the flatland below,
The desert May-dance
Of quilted flowers and butterflies bursting briefly
From seeming barrenness.

Or the ancient redwood forest,
Cradle dance of strength and comfort,
Evergreen,
Maidenhair fern and fern of sword,
Sorrel, salal and skunk cabbage,

The mundane and unbusy banana slug,
Complete and unhurried,
Unworried, trusting and alert,
Gliding over a trail of slime
In earthly advance through the wild and fruitful garden,
Plentiful and lusciously sustaining berries,
The crimson-blooded thimble berry,
The ruby and black pearl jewel-drop huckleberries,
Blackberry, elderberry, salmonberry, gooseberry.

These are part of me and my nourishment,
An unending procession of plenty.
Every type of tree having its own signature of shape and form,
Of bark, of fragrance, of sticky pitch,
Of interior wood grain or vein, of flower or cone, of leaf or needle.
Or the very branch pattern and hanging leaf mosaic of
Each species, distinct from all others,
Shades of color, and hues,
Endless variety of trees and shrubs.
The awesome splendor
Of a multicolored hardwood forest in autumn,
Dancing,
On a single October blackberry leaf.
Ah, this is joy!

Movement around, within and above,
Dancing in us,
Are the varied and capricious dances of weather,
Rain, hail, fog, mist,
And clouds, ah yes, especially clouds.
Textures and timbres of white, gray and purple by day
And the crepuscular color dance of dawn and dusk,
New color dimensions of green and orange, pink, rose and rust,
Ever changing and rearranging in beauty,
Across the peaceful,
Inner sky,

Our body-barometer registering subtle changes
in atmospheric pressure,
Unlabored dancing.
Smooth, lyrical and flowing,
The cantabile cloud song.

Capering and cavorting,
Smiling, flitting and flirting together,
Let us consider the value of a single snowflake,
Inconsequential, insignificant, unnoticed to the
world,
Priceless in its unique creation,
Swirling down in its communal dance.
This is our dance.

And the world of sound,
Nature's Ode to Joy,
With the sacred cries of all earth's creatures:

Laughing loons, whooping cranes,
trumpeter swans,
Snorts of seals,
Bugle blasts of sea lions,
Plaintive porpoises, mourning doves,
Sighing whales, screaming gulls,
Brown bats and pocket gophers, wood rats and
meadow voles,
Deer mice and gray squirrels, gray foxes and
gray wolves,
Coyotes, marmots, prairie dogs.

Every creature singing,
Howling, humming, buzzing,
Vibrating in sound.

Go on, hovering honeybee,
Unknowingly fertilizing all you come in contact with,
Extravagant in your dance.
Go on, modest rosebud,
Shyly taking several days,
Unfolding to flower,
In your elegant ballet so natural.

Meanwhile... in the heavens,
A hermit crab nebulae patiently unfurls,
And ever so much slower,
Creeps across the galaxies.

Countless moons waxing and waning through epic time,
Even rocks realizing their fluid dance-nature over geologic time.
One symphonic fabric of life
Covering the peopled planet,
Vibrations of sound and light,
Of uniqueness and mutuality,
Wholeness,
Holiness,
Uninjuredness,
Life-inhabited matter reflecting,
Chanting within and chanting without.

Allow the movement now to move you,
Meant now to move you,
Allow the movement now...
I shut my mouth
And close my eyes.
The conventions and conditions of my blessed personality
Are quieted.
The boundaries I thought I had are surprisingly loosened,
And the inner-earth, Rite of Spring, comes alive.
A creation dance,
Birthing, not boasting,
Pulsing, convulsing,
Inner earthling abundantly giving birth to
Loving worldling,
Value unreckonable, incalculable, inestimable.
Sacred earth and sacred body,
Holy natural scripture open to the world,
Abandon yourself to the dance,
Which, when without anxiety,
Is so kind,
With hope and respect and purpose,
With joy and caring and courage.
And forgiveness.

We dance for ourselves,
And help set others free.
(Or maybe just irritate them.)

Our dance of respect and pardon
Being fleetingly judged,
Before defenses are dismissed
And transformed to love.

Perhaps this angry bystander
Is, in his deepest being,
Something helpless that calls for help from us.

Regardless, we dance,
Not for effect,
Sometimes alone, sometimes in community.
My dance is my gift.
(Even if you don't see it that way.)
The joyful practice of dance is for all of us,
As is the practice of loving,
One of the arts by which we become unified
and complete,
Our gift, our birthright, our calling to integrity,
A vehicle by which we become human.

We dance and sing the one and only earthsong.

There is an urge, a drive, a purpose
And an accountability as an adult,
To sail out from my narrow everyday self,
My immediate family self, my professional self,
My personality who I thought I was,
Whether of smiling or of disagreeable
appearance,
Mask of falseness if it covers the completeness
within,
The urge, the drive, the purpose,
To find sympathy and connection in greater
spheres.

We are connected,
Whether we recognize it or not,
With our forebears, our children, our brothers
and our sisters,
Our loved ones, our adversaries and all life.
To be whole calls us in this direction.

An old-timer said,
"We will have to account to God
For all the good things our eyes beheld,
But which we refused to enjoy."
We, dance partner with me now,
Are gifts to each other,
Gifts from grace,
Brought to complete each other and make us whole.
Each dance and dancer
Related to
Each other dance and dancer,
Yet unique.
Each beautiful swirling individual
Reflecting the wonderful possibilities of the universe.

Make the dance your own,
That is to say, divine,
Bringing forth what is within,
And has always been,
To be visible plain as day.

The miniature gesture,
Part of a bigger dance,
Flexible, responding, yielding, resilient,
At peace with the world, with all beings,
With one's innards.

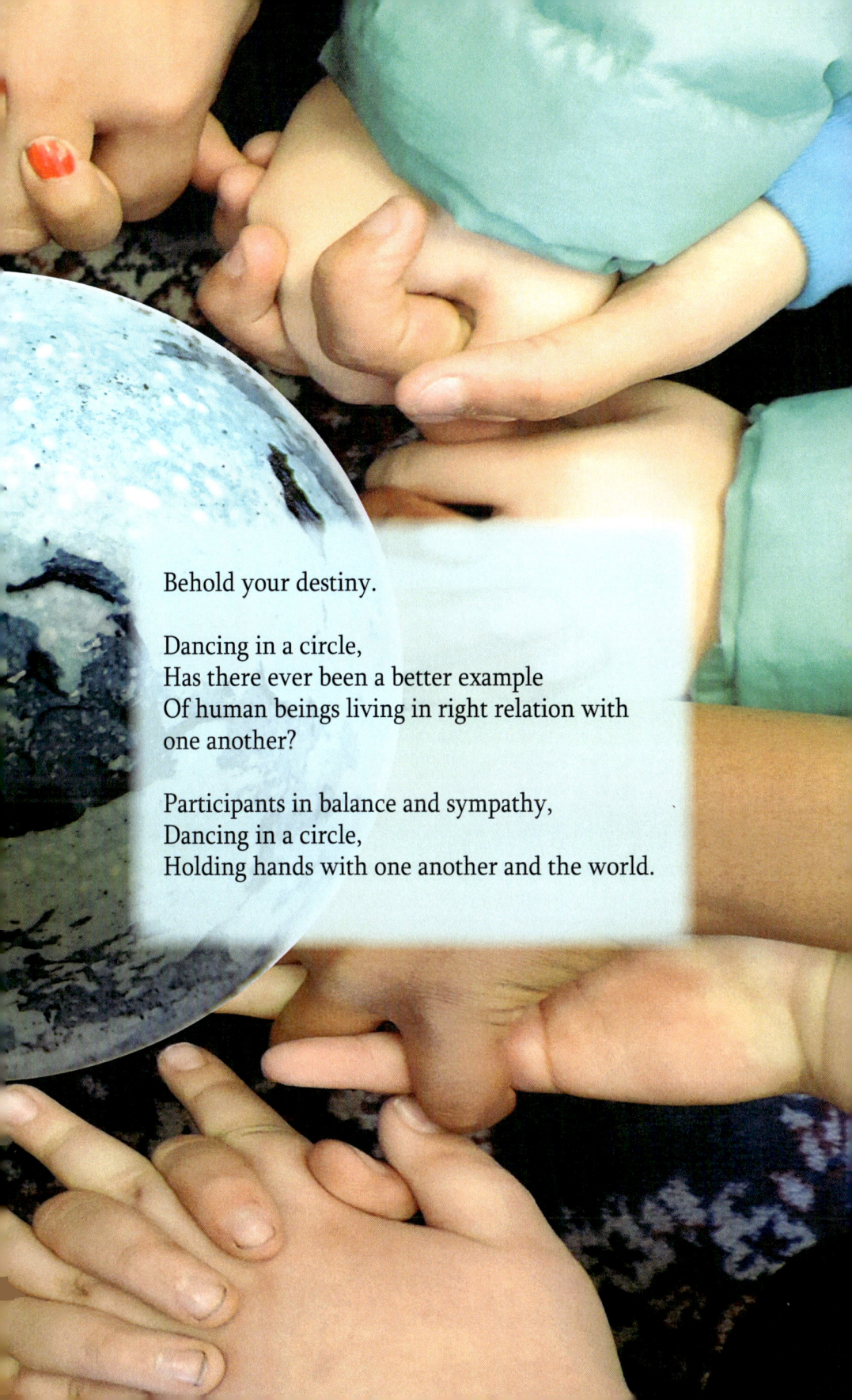

Behold your destiny.

Dancing in a circle,
Has there ever been a better example
Of human beings living in right relation with
one another?

Participants in balance and sympathy,
Dancing in a circle,
Holding hands with one another and the world.

In tune, joyful order, harmonious interwovenness,
What is the unique feeling carried by this dance?
What is the unique transformative quality carried in this song?
Unseen rhythms and waves, leaving us changed,
For the better,
More whole, complete.
Is it possible that the experience of dance is so pleasant
That we are washed and healed of our hurts?

A circle,
Strands of love
Connecting all,
Coming together
And passing on,
Carrying what was given
And passing on,
More circles
Of widening ripples and rounds.

Our dance is creative work,
Expressing spirituality as a force,
Which makes things happen.
Little, tiny things.

To understand the meaning
Of this pile of hopeful words,
Throw them all away,
Give yourself a smile,
And dance,
Please,
Now.

New dance,
   New dance partner,
      We pause in each other's eyes,

        Basking in the beautiful sunlight.
       Safe at last,
         But for a moment.
      There is no resting-place, no security.

Dance fellow, we need to stand before each other,
  To meet and accept each other,
    Grow beyond ourselves,
     Become each other's gift.

I am charmed to make your acquaintance.
 This short while,
   Let us be together, unfold together,
    Our parallel lives reflecting,
      Witnessing each other's unfolding.
     At this moment
       There is immortality.

Let us unfold each other in light,
 As we watch divinity unfolding.

The gifts of my heart I give to
you and to the whole world.
Will you bless my presence and
my disclosures as I bless yours?
Will you bless your own?
Oh, you who I dance with now,
I give you myself,
Free and un-ownable,
In beauty and nakedness,
Mystery, courage and trust.
We are given these dear bodies
To explore and grow beyond
these dear bodies.

We are related
By blood and attraction.
We are each the one
We have been looking for.

You are such a part of me,
Touching me with your
warmth and beauty.
Open your heart and pour
it forth
That I may receive it in equal
love and gladness.

Oh beautiful face,
Alive with body — clean and free in graceful
movement.
Perfect body, beautiful body,
Animated by
Perfect spirit, beautiful spirit.

Let us smile or not smile; it is the same,
Looking into each other's shining eyes
From this momentary world,
A bridge through the ages,
A soul-connection with the Ancients.

What is the name we put on the invisible power
That is transmitted through the eyes?
Between dance partners,
Between infant child and loving parent,
Or the innumerable expressions
Of eye aspect throughout the day,
Which inform and nourish all those we come in contact with,
Even the most aged and disabled of people,
Especially the most aged and disabled of people.
They feed us, those whose lifetimes have been filled,
Not by staring blankly at lifeless images on the wall,
Not by emulating lifeless personages projected on the screen,
But by soaking up the beauties of the world,
By making eye contact with real people,
And by listening to true humans.

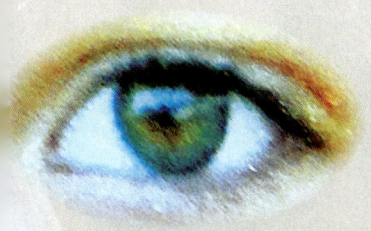

Why name the power of the eyes?
Let it be magic, let it be pleasant, let it be not difficult.
The child craves, creates, reflects the parent's smile,
And passes it on in the smile-dance with all others,
Family, friends and people around the globe,
Smiles that reach toward the future
And back through all of the ages,
To the dawn of time,
Entering the timeless dance of soul-seeing.

For now though, in joy, we are dancing,
Savoring the sweet viscous moment while knowing it will soon die,
Grieving even in the midst of the dance.
Thank you, you have done so much for me.

And so, let the life-dance of freedom begin.
Or rather say,
Let the love-dance continue,
The dance that can't be stopped,
Unceasing, unavoidable,
Inevitable, ineluctable,
Insurgent, insistent,
Inexorable, insuppressible, insurmountable,
Incorruptible, invincible, illimitable.

From molten space matter,
To primordial sea soup,
To the brotherhood and sisterhood of all creatures,
Abiding life inherently dancing forth,
Incredible, lovely and beautiful.

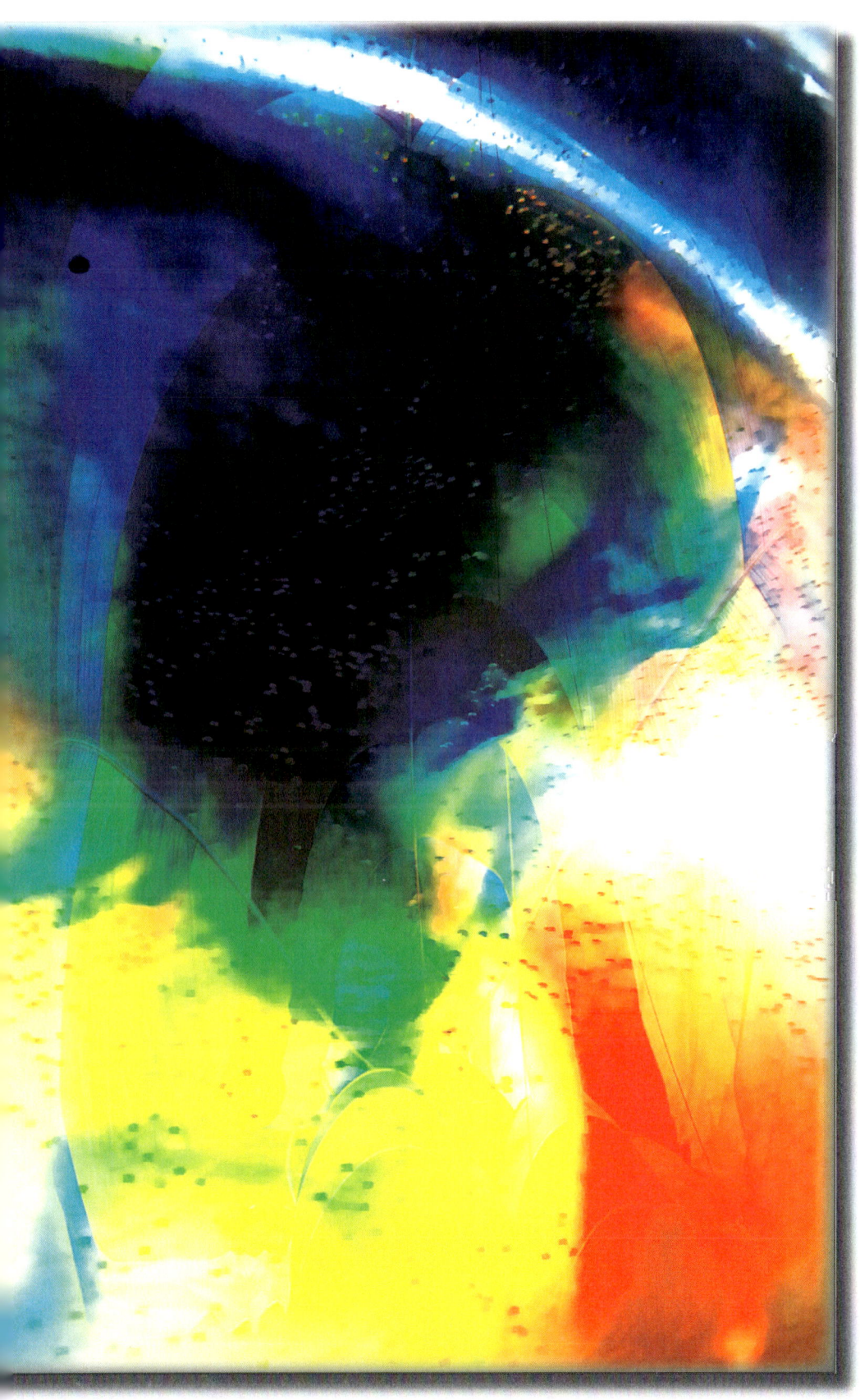

DETAILS OF PHOTOGRAPHS
(by page)

Cover Photo: Jacoby Creek

Front Inside Cover Photos:

    (Top Panoramic) Arcata Community Forest (photo by CM Phillips)

    (Bottom Panoramic) Redwood National Park, Prairie Creek (photo by CM Phillips)

i.	Infinity tattoos
vi.	Greetings & thanks
1.	Trillium, Jacoby Creek, Bayside
2-3.	Mill Creek waterfall, McKinleyville
4.	Great egret, Elk River Slough, Eureka
5.	Great blue heron, Arcata Marsh
6-7.	Big Lagoon (photo by CM Phillips)
8-9.	Sunset, Dry Lagoon
10.	Pacific tree frog, McKinleyville (photo by CM Phillips)
11.	California newt, Mattole River, Petrolia
13.	View through old growth redwood log, Arcata Community Forest
14-15.	Lost Coast, Petrolia
16.	Setka the wolf-hybrid, Samoa (photo by CM Phillips)
19.	Lichen on fence post, Elk River
20.	Rhododendron petals on sidewalk, Arcata

22-23. (Top Panoramic) Pelicans, cormorants, & godwits on Franklin Klopp Lake, Arcata Marsh (photo by CM Phillips)

23. (Bottom Right) Pelican taking flight, Arcata Marsh (photo by CM Phillips)

24. Starfish & sea anemone at Luffenholz Beach, Trinidad (Photo by CM Phillips)

27. Water droplets on leaf

28. Angel Ranch cabin, Korbel

31. Spruce tree growing over old growth redwood stump, Arcata Community Forest

32-33. Canada geese at the Arcata Marsh superimposed over Palco Marsh wetlands

34-35. (Top Panoramic) Mattole riverbank

35. Bronze Chinook Salmon (photo by Thomas Dunklin)

36-37. (Top Conglomerate Panoramic) Roosevelt elk herd at Gold Bluff Beach, Prairie Creek Redwoods State Park (photos by David Wilder Pickart-Jain & Peter K. Jain)

37. Agate, Agate Beach, Patrick's Point State Park

38. Douglas iris, Arcata Community Forest

40. Skunk cabbage, Prairie Creek Redwoods State Park

41. (Top from left to right): Thimble Berry, Huckleberries, Blackberries, Elderberries, Salmonberry, Arcata Community Forest
(Bottom) Banana slug, Arcata Community Forest

43. Blackberry leaf in fall color, Mad River

44-45. Clouds over St. Joseph's Church, Blue Lake

46. (Top left) Molting elephant seal pup (a rarity in our county), Trinidad (photo by CM Phillips)

46-47. (Bottom Panoramic) Harbor seals near the mouth of the Mad River (photo by CM Phillips)

49. Honeybee, McKinleyville (photo by CM Phillips)

50. Full moon through maple trees, Arcata

51. Seashell, Manilla

52-53. Amanita muscaria, Sequoia Park, Eureka

54-55. Farmer's Market, Arcata Plaza

56. Woodley Island Marina, Eureka

57. Lighthouse & harbor, Trinidad

58-59. Farmstead near Freshwater

60-61. Children holding hands

62. Waves at sunset, Luffenholz Beach, Trinidad (photo by CM Phillips)

64-65. Humboldt beads & beach beauties

66-67. Inukshuk sculptures superimposed over Stone Lagoon

68-69. Driftwood adorned in sunset, Dry Lagoon

70. Covered bridge over Elk River

71. Hammond Bridge over Mad River

72-73. Eyes superimposed over abalone shell

75. Children on Redwood Creek

77. Colored dye superimposed over hot air balloon (Kneeland)

81. Thanks

82-83. Back Inside Cover Photos (left to right):
Spring daffodils, Arcata Bottoms
Baker Beach in summer
Freshwater barn in fall color
Redwood forest in winter, Liscomb Hill

"Dancers are the messengers of the gods."
— *MARTHA GRAHAM*

"Before my life is over, may I have sung the song of my soul." — *HAZRAT INAYAT KHAN*